EXPLORING SHELTER ISLAND
A Book For Curious Young Visitors

A Publication of Milk & Cookies Press
a J. Boylston & Company, Publishers imprint

MILK &
COOKIES
PRESS
TM

EXPLORING SHELTER ISLAND
A Book For Young Visitors
Text Copyright © 2022 by Therése Palmiotto
Illustrations Copyright © 2022 by Samuel Palmiotto

J. Boylston & Company, Publishers
Manhanset House, Dering Harbor, NY 11965-0342
www.ibooksinc.com
ISBN: 978-1-899694-03-7
First edition, hardcover printing: Summer 2022
Library of Congress Cataloging-in-Publication Data available

EXPLORING SHELTER ISLAND

A Book For Curious Young Visitors

written by Therése Palmiotto
illustrated by Samuel Palmiotto

MILK &
COOKIES
PRESS
™

New York
Habent sua fata libelli

North

South

POOL

Ride the ferry over
It isn't very far.
Less than a ten-minute journey
On foot, bike or car.

S.I.

Enjoy a day at the beach
There are quite a few to choose.

Read the Shelter Island Reporter
To stay up to date on town news.

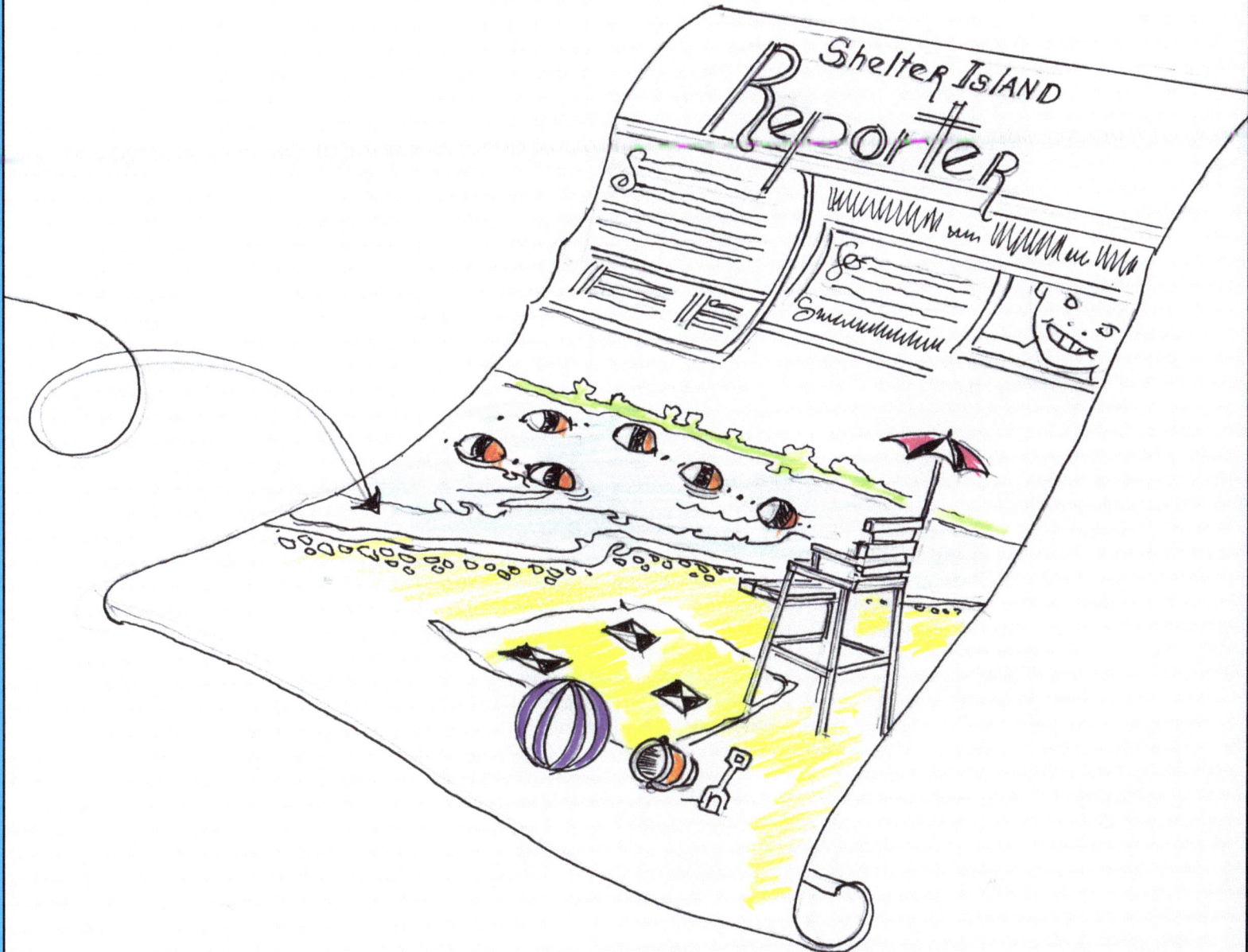

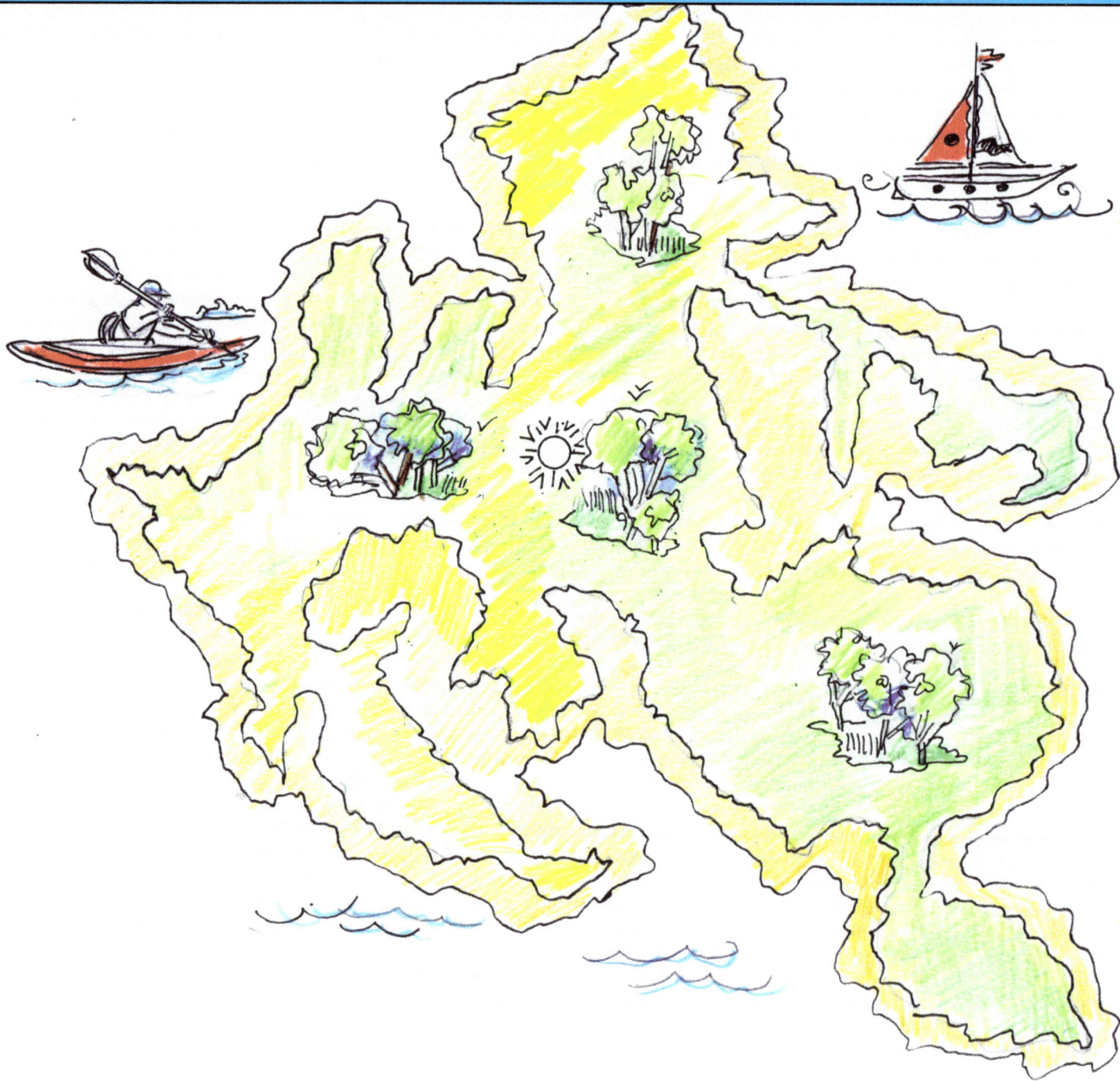

Turkeys, deer and fox
They all live here too.
You might see a blue heron
You'll be lucky if you do.

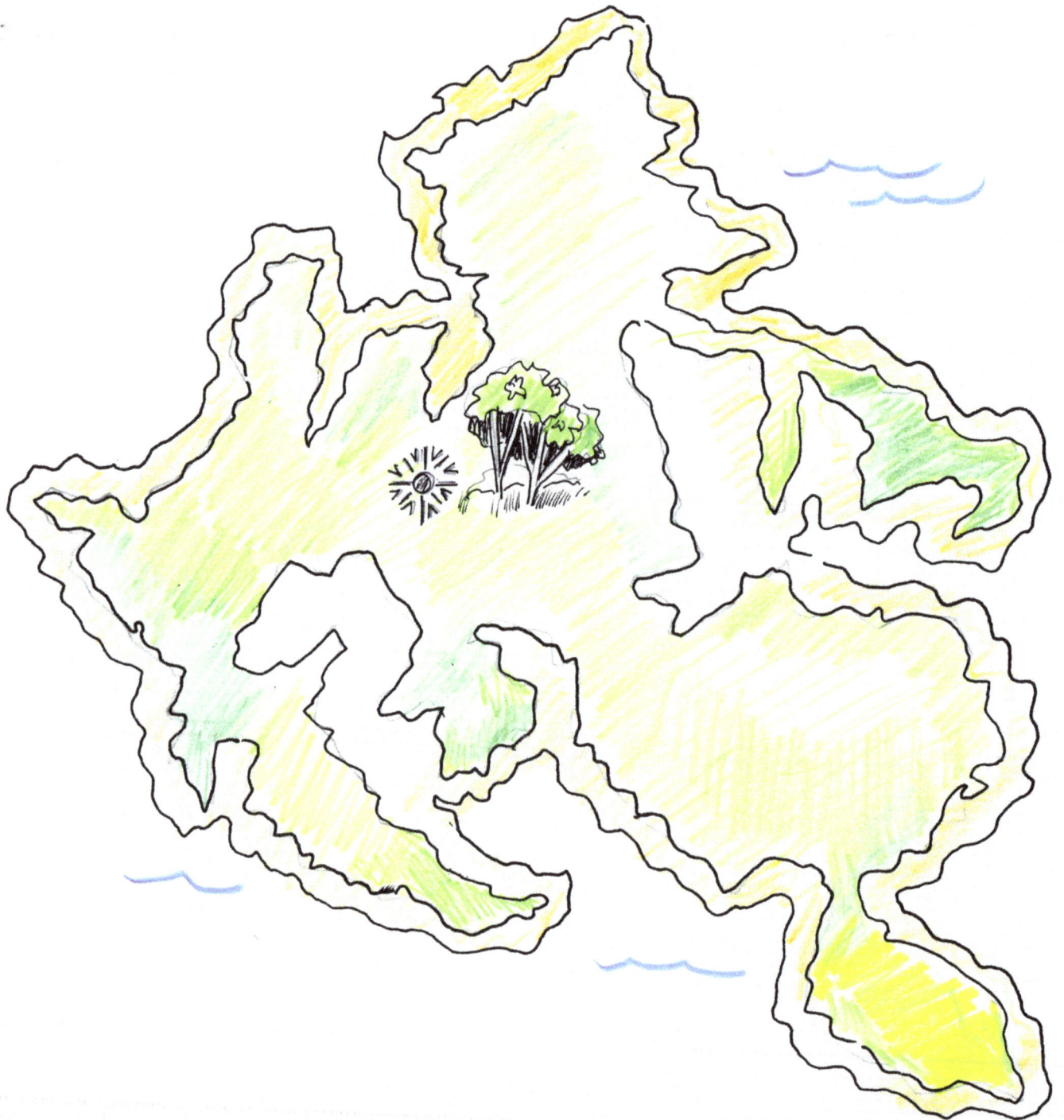

Keep an eye out on the road
When you're driving all around.
There may be turtles crossing
Let's keep them safe and sound.

Spend some time out on the water
Any way that you choose.

Kayak, boat or paddle board
You just can't beat the views.

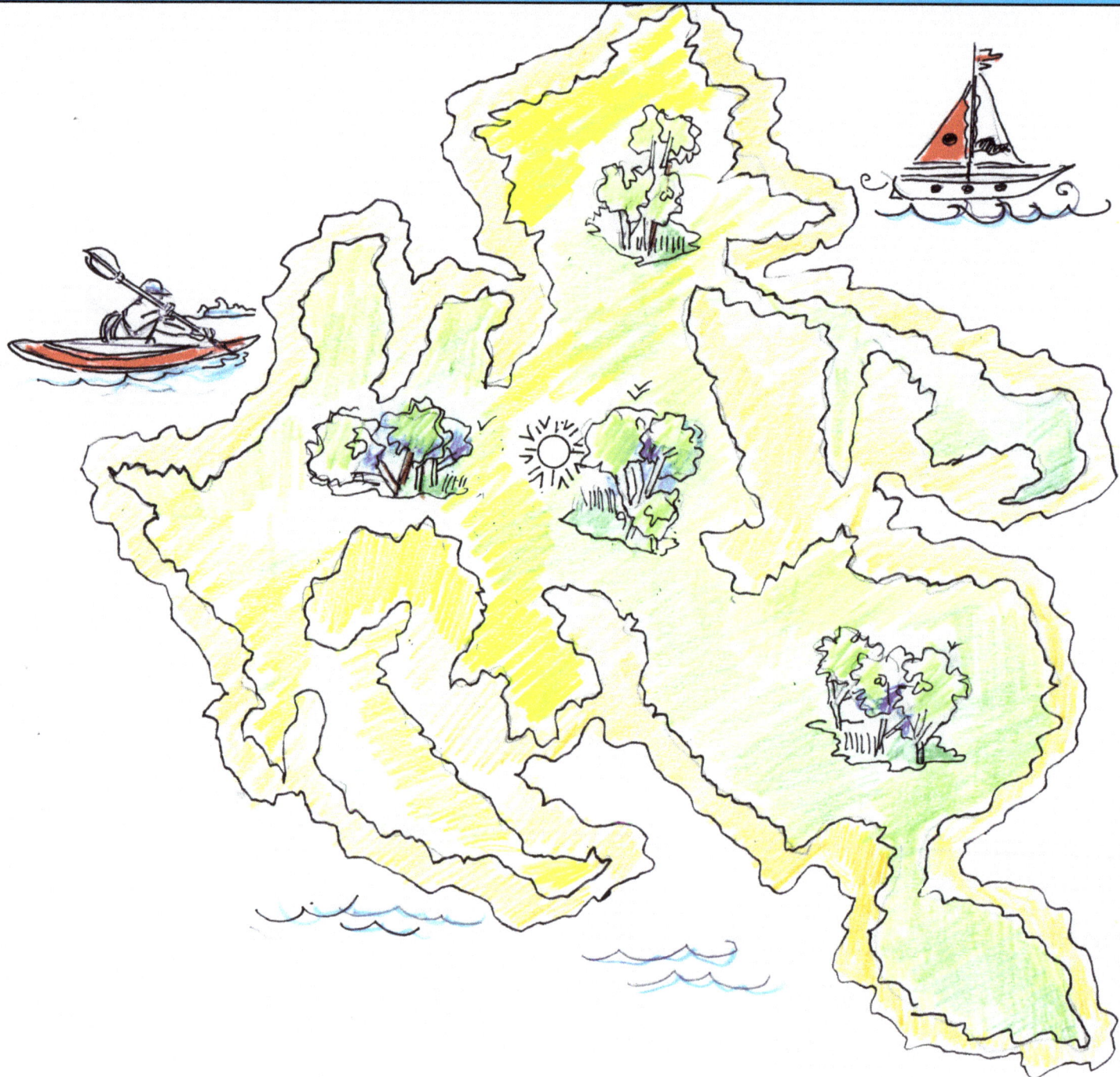

Listen for the ospreys
Watch them soaring through the sky.
They love living on the island
And it's obvious why.

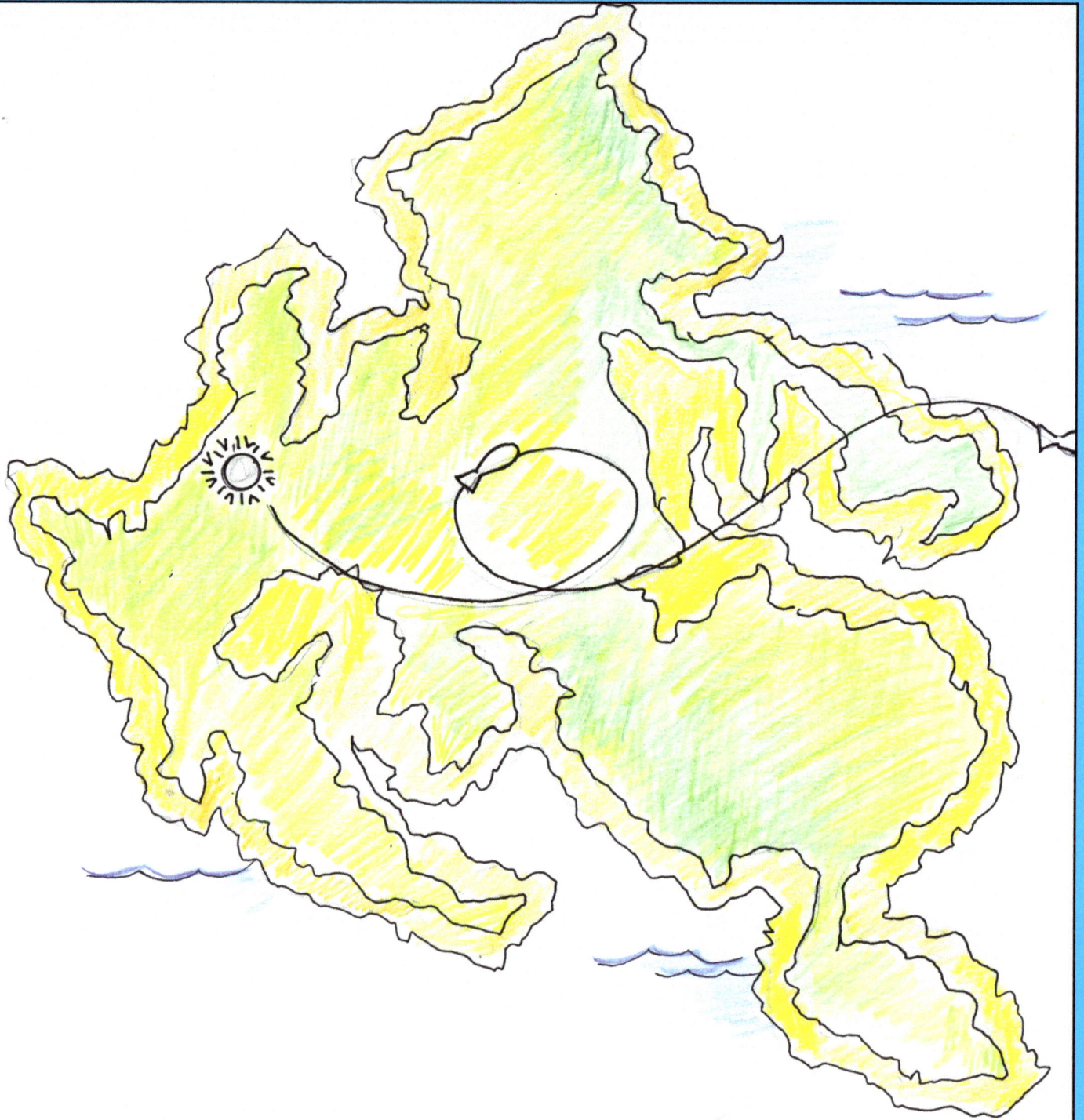

Get your fishing rod ready
See if the fish will bite.
Porgies, bass & snappers
Reel them in without a fight.

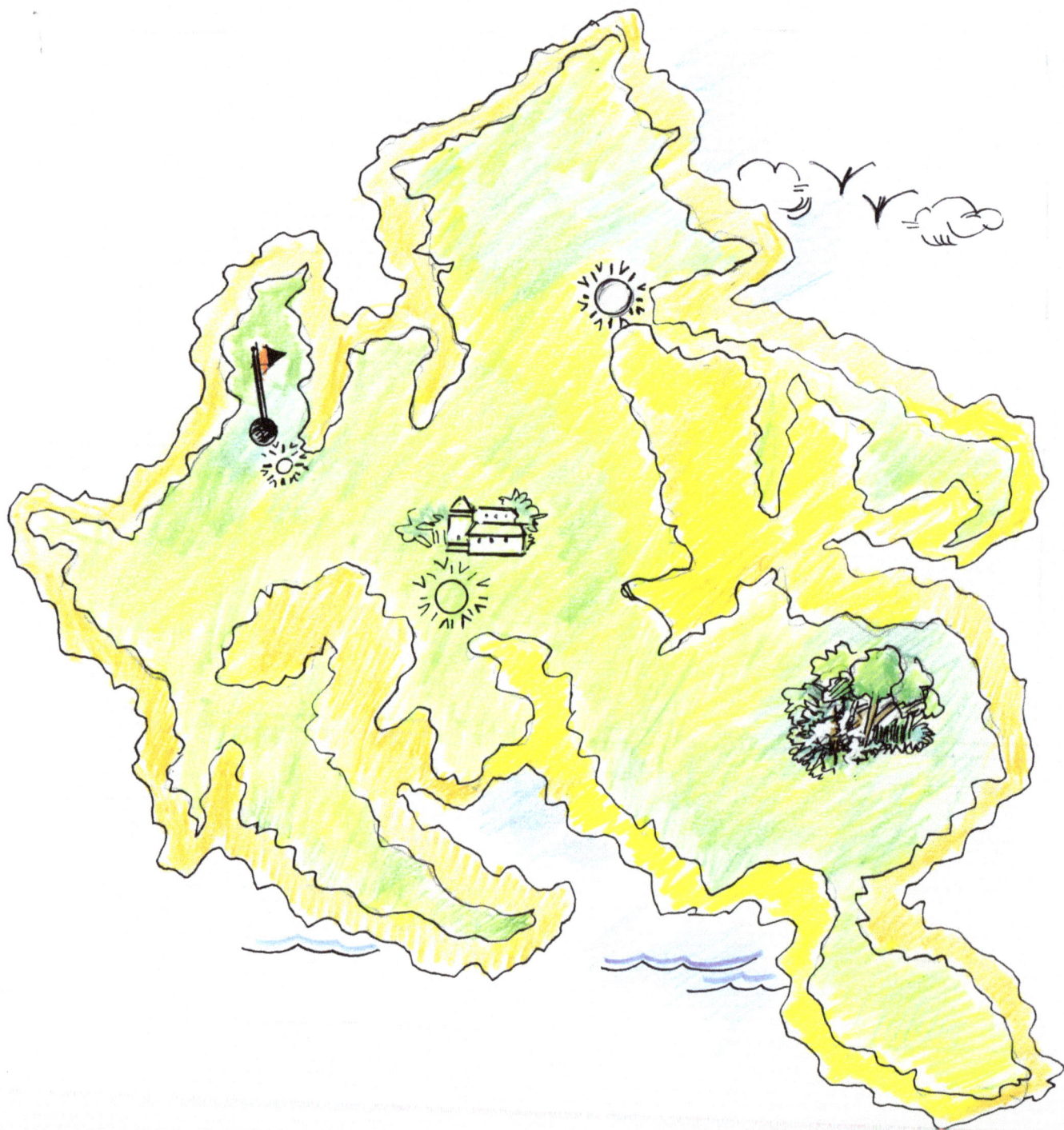

A round of golf at 'Goat Hill'
Is a worthy activity to note.
Follow up your tee-time
With a meal at the Flying Goat.

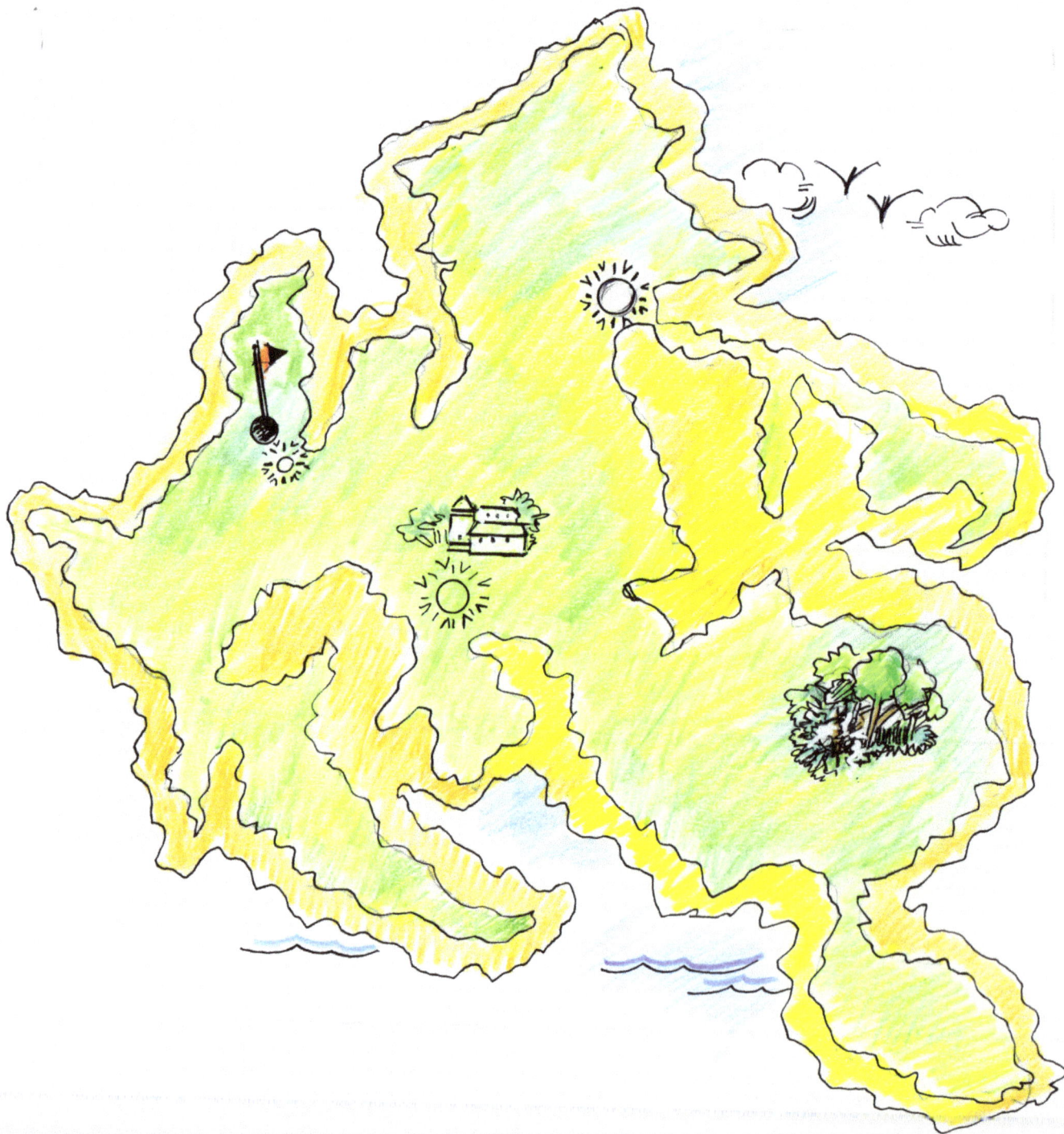

Want to learn more about the island?
The Havens House is where you go.
The Historical Society knows everything about it
And can tell you what you want to know.

If it's quiet, peace and calm,
Natural beauty you want to observe;
Get on your hiking shoes,
And visit Mashomack Preserve.

Manhanset

SHELTER ISLAND

The Manhanset tribe
Were the native people of the land.
If you do a little searching,
You might find an artifact in the sand.

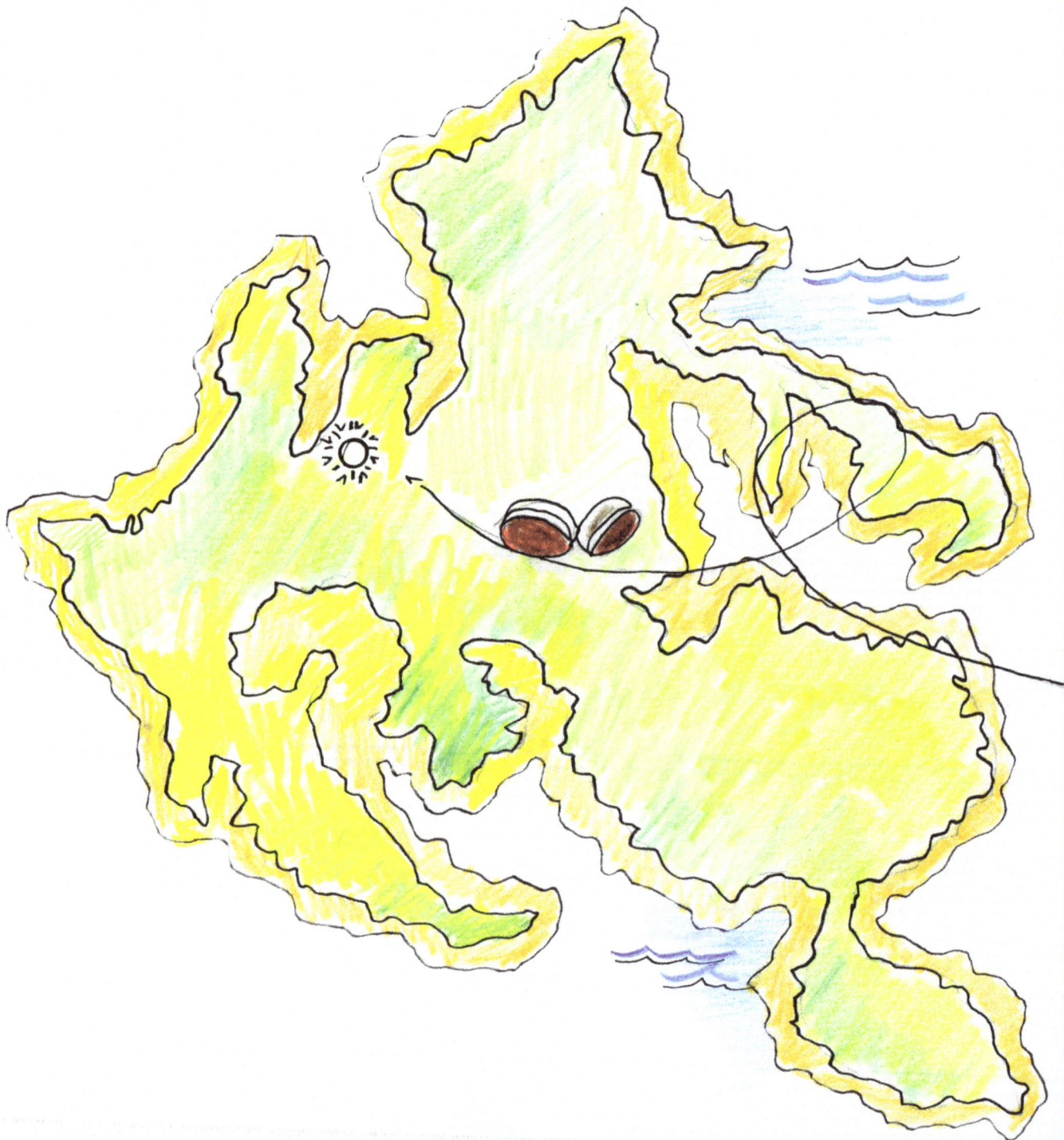

Marvel Victorian houses
Do some shopping in the Heights.
Enjoy a cookie or a latte
And dine outside when it is nice.

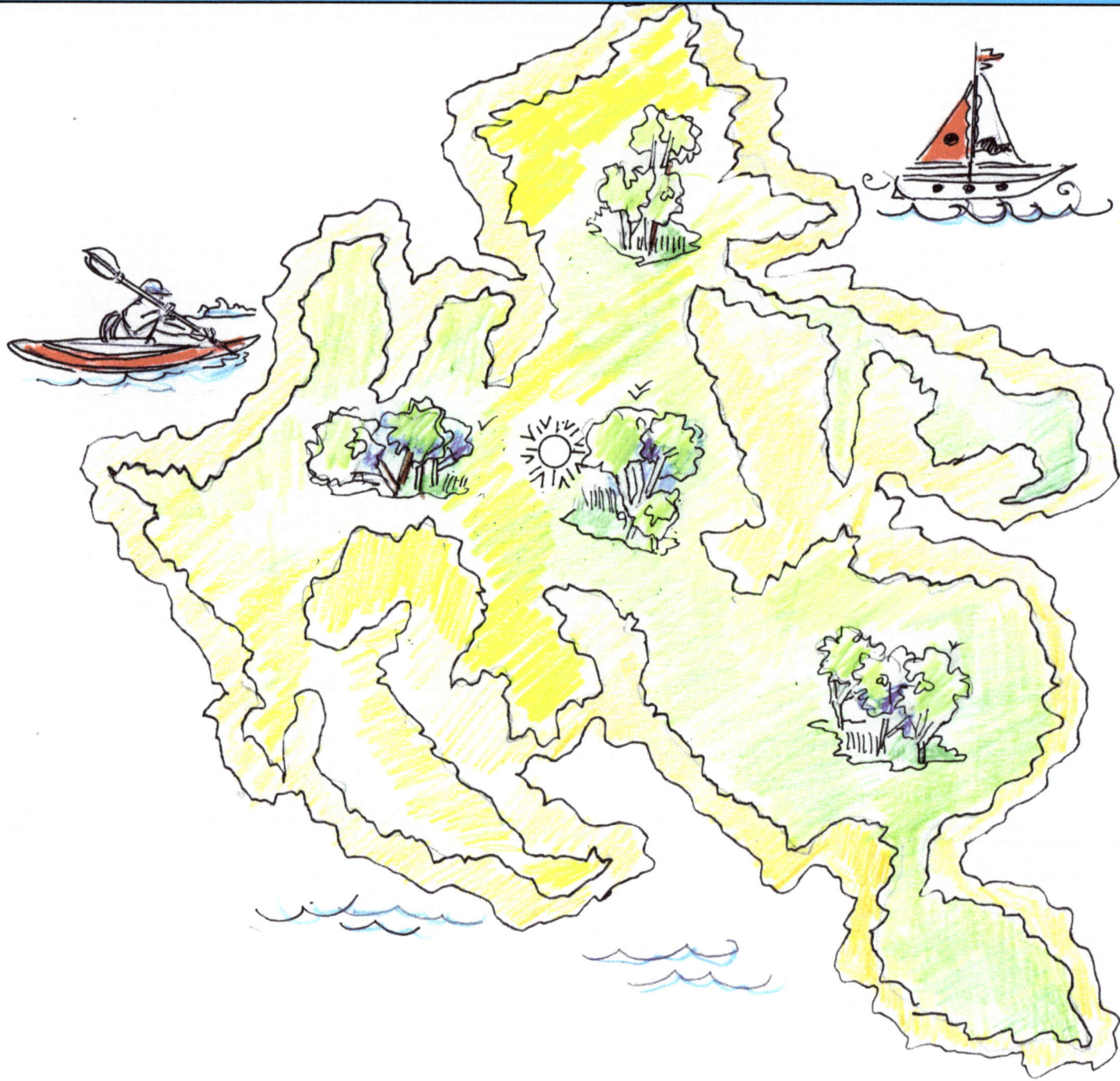

Visit Sylvester manor
For its historical charm.
Once a slave-holding plantation—
Now an organic educational farm.

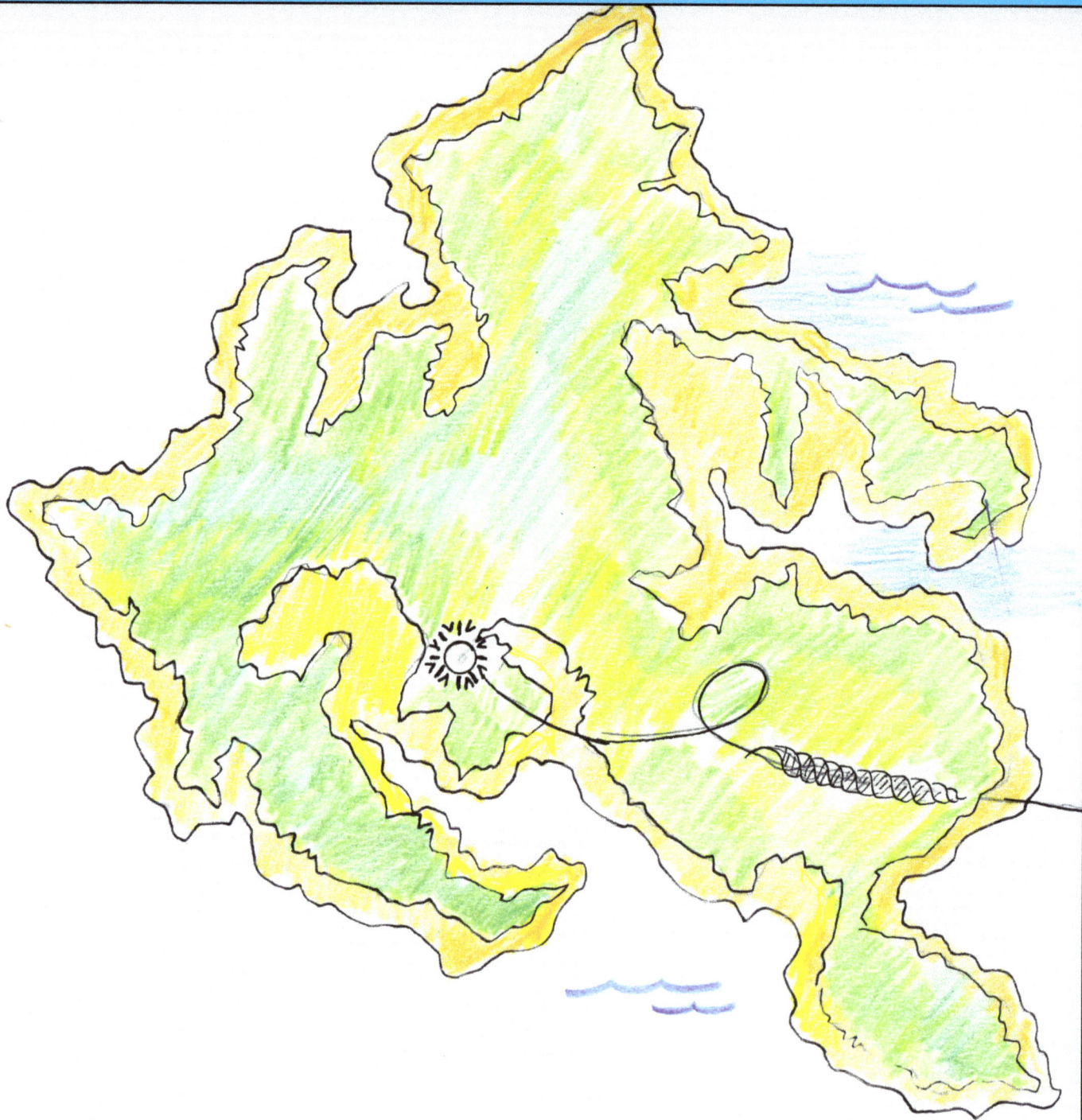

LORD SHIPYARD.
1861

Try to find the marker
For Lord Ship Yard on Menantic.
Where a schooner built for the Napoleonic Wars
Was sent across the Atlantic.

S.I.

A perfect day on Shelter Island
Ends with a glorious sunset.
Enjoy a beach picnic or bonfire
To mark a day you won't forget.

Milk & Cookies Press
Manhanset House
Dering Harbor, New York 11965-0342
www.ibooksinc.com

www.IngramContent.com

For sales in the UK and Europe please contact our distributor,
Gazelle Book Services
Falcon House, Queens Square
Lancaster, LA1 1RN, UK
Tel: (01524) 68765 Fax: (01524) 63232
stef@gazellebooks.co.uk

www.ingramcontent.com/pod-product-compliance
Lightning Source LLC
Chambersburg PA
CBHW040853100426

42813CB00015B/2787